Denis Mitchell
Ascending Forms

Artist in his studio c 1970

Introduction

This is the first time a significant group of sculptures by Denis Mitchell has been shown since his memorial retrospective at the Glynn Vivian Museum and Art Gallery in 1994. A variety of works in stone, slate and wood together with a large group of bronzes have been chosen to be exhibited alongside the exhibition of Wilhelmina Barns-Graham's works *Movement and Light: Imag(in)ing Time*. Wilhelmina and Denis and his wife Jane were 'honest' friends from the early 1940s when she arrived from Edinburgh. Denis had come to St Ives in the 1930s from Swansea and began developing his painting career whilst working as a market gardener with his brother.

Denis and Wilhelmina, together with John Wells and Bernard Leach, were in close rapport as artists and supported each other as the younger generation involved with others in setting up the Penwith Gallery. Denis was a very calm, collected and diplomatic individual and when artistic disputes took place, he was adept in negotiating the politics of place. A very popular and respected figure, he later became Chairman of the Penwith Society where he held a pivotal role in the evolving arts scene in St Ives.

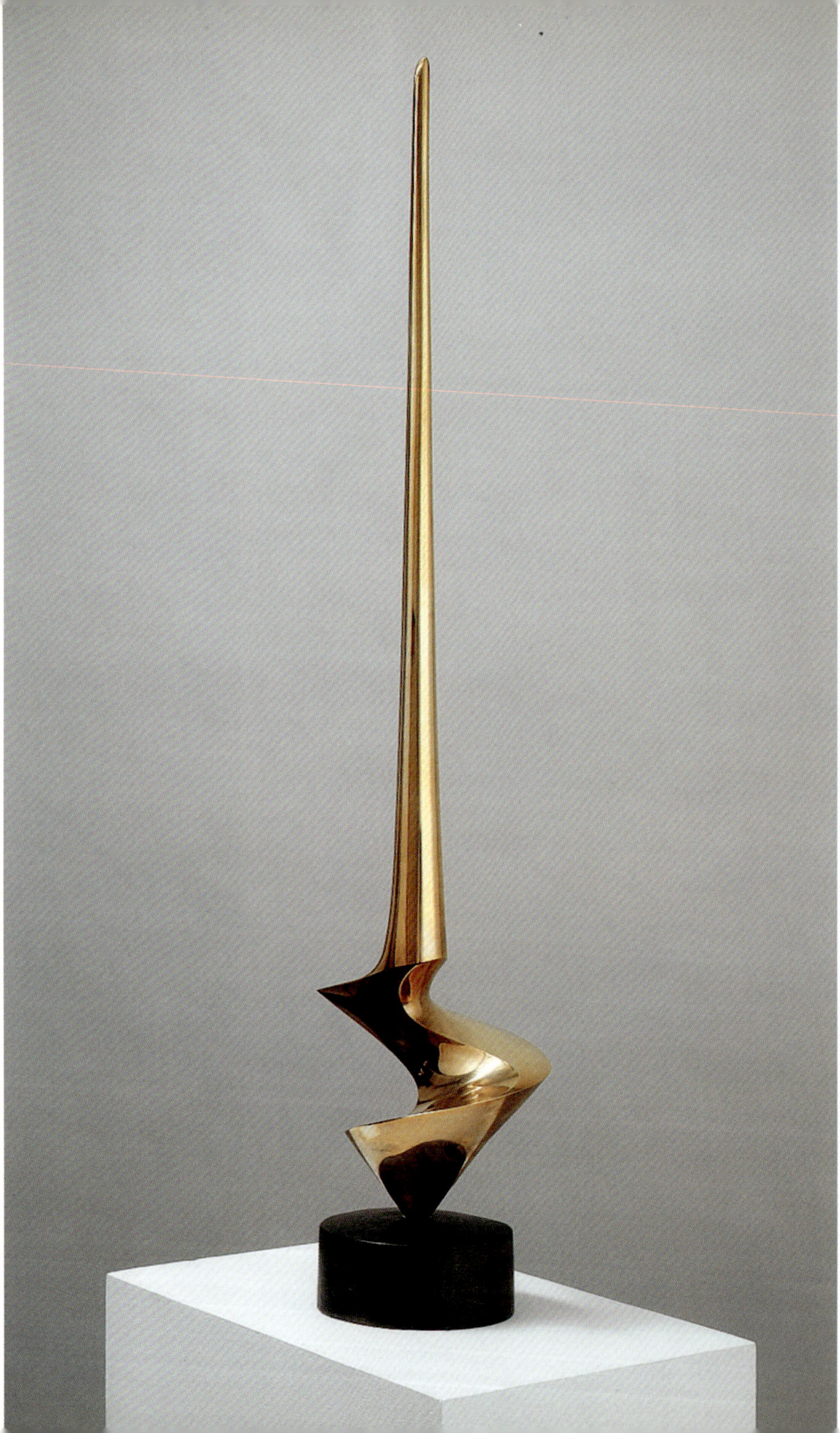

Thrust 1992 (second cast)
Bronze 123.2 x 28.5 x 21 cm
Courtesy of Heller Collection

In April 2000, I visited John Wells at Trewarveneth School in Newlyn. There I was privileged to sit with John and whilst talking, observe Denis Mitchell's work all around us in the studio (which was next door to John's). Denis' studio had a comfortable couch and gas fire and John often received his guests there. It was this rare sighting of a treasure trove of a room packed with sculptures, drawings and photographs that led me to make visual connections with Wilhelmina's works almost five years later.

Sara Hughes, in her thoughtful and historically interesting essay, gives insight into Denis Mitchell's approach in the St Ives context. We are also grateful to the sculpture conservation team in Tate for their support in preparing the works for exhibition. Our warm thanks go to a large number of lenders including Jennifer Seton, The Stanley Picker Private Collection, the Heller Collection, George and Ann Dannatt, Frank Manzi and Flowers East who have been generous in releasing their works to be shown to the public. Lastly, we are particularly indebted to the Mitchell family, particularly Jane and Denise, for facilitating the links between works and collectors to help us make this exhibition.

Susan Daniel-McElroy Director Tate St Ives

Turning Form 1959
Bronze 164 x 27 x 31 cm
Tate

Denis Mitchell Ascending Forms

After his departure from Barbara Hepworth's Trewyn Studio in 1959, Denis Mitchell wrote to friend and mentor Ben Nicholson in Switzerland to thank him for his continued encouragement. Whilst he admitted the decade working as Hepworth's chief assistant had proved invaluable, he was at last steadily progressing with his own ideas, confiding the impossibility of casting in bronze without Nicholson's financial support.[1] The money had come as recompense for the repairs Mitchell had made to one of Nicholson's seminal 1930s white reliefs he much admired.

Following the production of Mitchell's first small bronze *Zawn* in 1958, a series of rising vertical works emerged, including *Turning Form* (1959). The undulating polished surface that interplays line, space, light and form, is partly indebted to John Wells' painting of 1950, *Aspiring Forms*. Wells' Constructivist composition of interlocking parabolic curves was the initial catalyst for Mitchell's further exploration of bronze's potential. These ambitious works immediately enlightened Mitchell's pursuit of personal sculptural forms, in a medium Barbara Hepworth was yet to fully embrace.

1 Tate Gallery Archive: Letters from Denis Mitchell to Ben Nicholson TAG: 8717.1.2.2940-66A

Hepworth's tutelage had bestowed upon Mitchell an uncompromising love of pure form and a firm attachment to carving. By the late 1950s he had already exhibited many accomplished works in wood, stone and slate relief. However, his discovery of the sand-cast bronze, a cheaper yet cruder method of casting, imposed a satisfying simplicity on his evolving repertoire of abstract forms. The gruelling task of hand-finishing allowed Mitchell time to engage with the formal and conceptual progression of his ideas by virtue of this intuitive mode of working.

By 1969 Patrick Heron, in a foreword to his solo exhibition at Marjorie Parr Galleries, London declared Mitchell 'the only important British sculptor junior to Moore and Hepworth who has never deserted the carved or hand-cut form as the sole vehicle of expression', admiring the persistence, integrity and enduring quality Mitchell offered against the backdrop of Minimalist and Pop Art trends.

The exhibition of Mitchell's work at Tate St Ives draws together eleven of his celebrated bronzes originally designed or cast between 1959 and 1971, with the addition of four works in wood, slate and stone from 1974 and 1985. Chosen to be shown alongside the works of Wilhelmina Barns-Graham (1912-2004), the exhibition highlights the evolution of Mitchell's carved forms from 1959 and reminds us of his role in the progression of Modernism in St Ives. Pre-dating the arrival of the 'first generation' Modernists Barbara Hepworth (1903-75), Ben Nicholson (1894-1982) and Naum Gabo (1890-1977), Mitchell observed the changing nature of the artists' colony for almost

63 years. In addition to his tenure with Hepworth, his initial experiences of eking a living from the land in pre- and post-war Cornwall, and the artistic relationships he made, were implicit to determining his aesthetic sensibilities.

Born in 1912 in Wealdstone, Middlesex, Denis Mitchell spent the first seventeen years of his childhood in Mumbles, Swansea. Separated from his father, his mother moved Mitchell and his older brother Endell to live with their uncle on the Gower Peninsula. On leaving grammar school there was little impetus in post-war Swansea for Mitchell to train as an artist. Whilst it was clear to him that this was his vocation, his early creative training was acquired from making theatre sets for the amateur dramatics society and undertaking odd jobs at a commercial art studio.

By 1930, the depression had left Mitchell struggling to find work. Despite enrolling in evening classes at Swansea School of Art, the aspiring artist and his brother accepted the offer to renovate an aunt's cottage at Balnoon, just outside St Ives. On their move to the Cornish coastal town, they could make their livelihoods by cultivating a market garden and in the milieu of the renowned artists' colony, both young men would have a serious opportunity to paint.

The rise of the St Ives Society of Artists in the late 1920s championed the landscape and marine traditions of *pléin air* painting. Mitchell became a particular admirer of the painter John Park and made many pictorial landscape studies in his spare time.[2] But his relationship with the landscape through gardening and painting was to take on another dimension when he was drafted to work at Geevor tin mine in St Just during the Second World War. It proved a

2 Interview between Denis Mitchell and Roger Slack c.1985 in archive of the artist's estate.

profound visual and philosophical experience. Mitchell often recalled the humility he felt when shovelling earth deep underground or singing hymns in the cathedral-like caverns at the base of the shaft before ascending to the top.[3]

A series of Mitchell's mining paintings were shown at the Castle Inn on Fore Street (then run by his brother Endell), alongside a growing circle of Modernists including Hepworth and Nicholson. By the late 1940s the 'Castle' had become a makeshift arts club for these radical contemporary artists pursuing international abstract trends. The hostility from the established figurative school of the St Ives Society of Artists, gave the 'Moderns' little opportunity to exhibit in the town. As a result, in 1949, the tavern hosted the inaugural meeting of the rival Penwith Society of Arts. Mitchell, along with Bernard Leach, Wilhelmina Barns-Graham and others was a founding member.

The Society, chaired by Mitchell in the mid 1950s, formalised the international context which was centring on St Ives. Such was its reputation and importance to the revival of post-war British art (fuelled in particular by the critical writings of Herbert Read and subsequently Patrick Heron), it continued to attract leading abstract artists to the town. Figures such as Victor Pasmore and William Scott were eager to exhibit in its new 'inclusive' gallery space. Mitchell's studio, a fish-loft a few doors along on Fore Street (which he had occupied since the early 1940s) also became popular for its coffee and artistic or social exchange for the resident and visiting artists.

Coupled with joining Hepworth's studio, this period marked Mitchell's development from figurative painter to abstract sculptor. Employed by Hepworth on the recommendation of Bernard Leach, he was initially engaged with

3 *Ibid*

Terry Frost and John Wells to work on her large commission for the Festival of Britain. Mitchell soon became, as he described 'Hepworth's hands', and quickly understood her vocabulary of forms. Hepworth had been positioned amongst the pre-war pioneers who were exploring open forms, including the Russian Constructivist Naum Gabo (who had settled in Carbis Bay during the war) and British sculptor Henry Moore. Her practice had continued in the 1950s to embody the values of 'truth to materials' alongside the Constructivist aims of engaging new dimensions of movement, light and space into sculpture. However, like many of her post-war contemporaries in St Ives, such as painters Wilhelmina Barns-Graham and Patrick Heron, her principles of abstraction were articulated by a personal response to the landscape.

Mitchell's context for development from 1949-59 was ostensibly internationally stimulated. He began exhibiting in London in small group shows and visited amongst others Heron and Moore. His diverse sculptural output during this decade draws from the broad range of elements constituent in St Ives Modernism and, in becoming an accomplished carver, he was able to test the potential of materials. His early works included drawings for sculpture and reliefs in slate or board which interplayed line, surface and depth. He also fabricated constructions in iron, brass and wood exploring the spatial relationships of geometric forms, whilst carving lyrical single forms in polished African hardwoods that evoked the figure or the natural world.

The sculptor's interest in non-western art could be seen in his collection of curios and African masks. It was a cultural reference which had provided new energy and ideas in Modernist sculpture from the early twentieth century and

Mitchell's admiration for pioneers like Constantin Brancusi was directly evident in works such as the totemic iroko wood figure *Arch Priest* exhibited at the Drian Gallery in 1958. However, previously in 1953, Ben Nicholson prompted the sculptor to see the exhibition of Mexican and pre-Colombian art at the Tate Gallery, London which he also cited as greatly influential to his practice.[4] Certainly, it may have prompted his decision to travel to Columbia in 1970. In a review of this renowned exhibition the critic C. A. Burland exclaimed, 'There is a great gulf between pre-Colombian iconography and our own customs yet we can all agree this is great sculpture...for this art of Mexico is an art to shake one out of complacency, and make one think how to express the beliefs of ones own time'.[5]

Mitchell's 'iconography' emerges from 1960 onwards, coinciding with his departure from Trewyn studio, when he took up teaching first in Penzance then at Redruth. The forms in bronze produced from this time particularly embody Mitchell's philosophy and craftsmanship, creating objects which Heron suggested in 1969 as both personally and universally relevant.

Following *Turning Form* in 1959, Mitchell's sculptures, such as *Gew Form* (1960) and *Landscape Form* (1960) suggest his experience of being in, and working on the land referencing bird, fish or organic forms. They also represent figures or recall the tools of his various trades, gardening, mining, fishing and carving[6] captured in *Thrust* (1960) (recast 1992), *Morvah* (1989)[7] and *Praze* (1964). Initially more narrative, the titles became arbitrary Cornish village and farm names, deliberately evading literal translation.

4 Artist statement exh.cat. *Denis Mitchell*, Glynn Vivian Art Gallery, 1979

5 Studio Magazine, June 1953, pp.188-193

6 See Tom Cross, *Painting the Warmth of the Sun*, Lutterworth Press, 1995, pp120-121

7 Both *Thrust* and *Morvah* were from original casts or designs made in the early 1960s; *Thrust* was originally cast in aluminium a material the artist experimented with at the time before reverting to bronze

Landscape Form 1960
Bronze 18.6 x 56.8 x 15.3 cm
Collection of George and Ann Dannatt

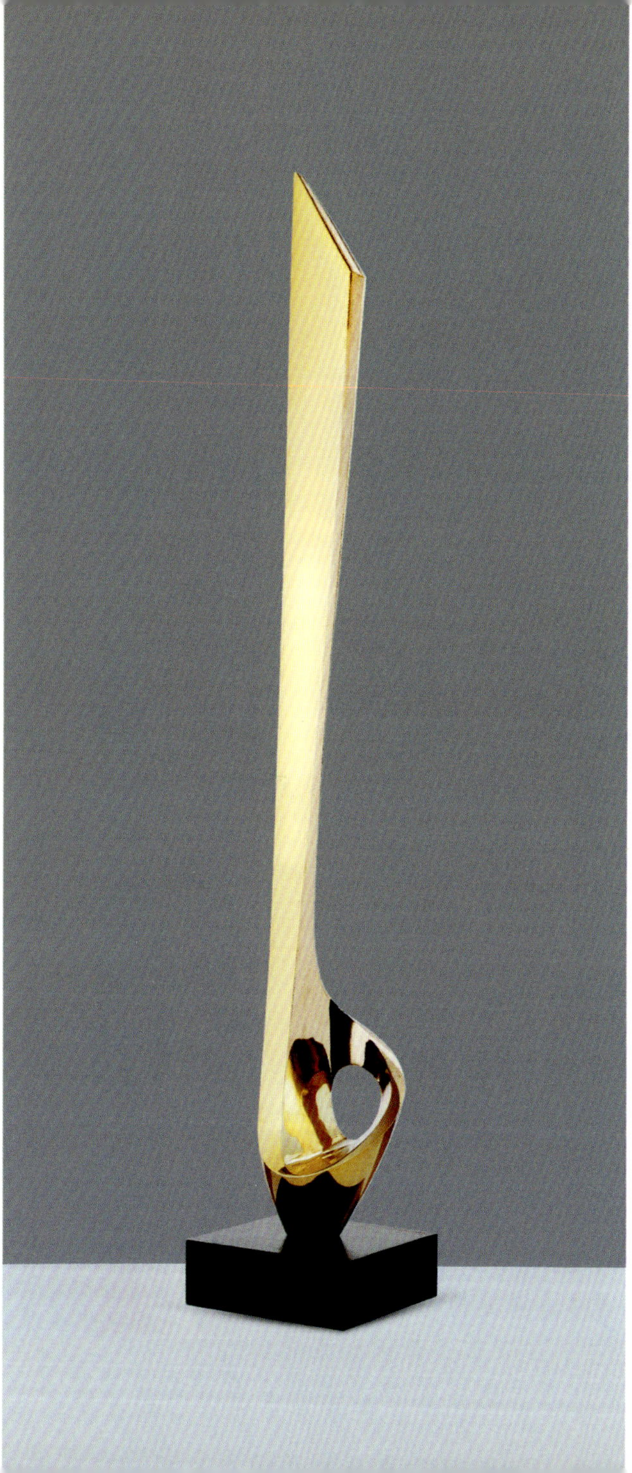

Opposite
Praze 1964
Bronze 191.8 x 27.9 x 28.6 cm
Tate

Right
Gew Form 1960
Bronze 33 x 12.7 x 7.6 cm
Collection of Jennifer Seton

Excavated solid forms, open ovals, two-pronged or columnar single forms typify this period; often two-sided or in relief, they are a progression from two-dimensional designs and many are heraldic in their presentation. Engaging with elements of Constructivist thinking, the objects incorporate space and bring light into solid mass. But the poetic balance of line, curve, form and subtle asymmetry in these significant forms register with the subconscious, conveying an innate vitality.

Operating on both a monumental and intimate scale, Mitchell exploits the inherent qualities of polished metal to articulate both physical and psychological dynamics in his work. For example, *Praze* has a transcendental quality as light moves up this architectonic single form, thus recalling the Gothic pillar or Mitchell's spiritual experience of ascending from the depths of the mines. *Thrust*, with its tapered column, denotes pure energy as light shoots through the tension of the coiled mass at the base. The organic *Gew Form*, signifies regeneration as the mirrored surface evokes life-force whilst prompting a visual exchange between the patinated interior and reflective exterior of the form.[8]

Often mounted on Delabole slate, the material is used to stage the activated space in and around the sculpture, essential to Mitchell's ongoing dialogue between the positive and negative aspects of form. In *Clowance* (1964) for example, encapsulated space becomes the single form held between the tensions of the vertical patinated 'prongs'. In other bronze works, the slate offers a grounding visual contrast to the elusiveness of their shine.

It is interesting that Mitchell chose not to achieve the surface through the quick-fix of chrome-plating; the shine is achieved simultaneously with the

8 See properties of shine discussed by Jon Wood in exh.cat *Shine: Sculpture and Surface* in the 1920s and '30s Henry Moore Institute Essays on Sculpture, Leeds, 2002 pp3-4 regarding associations with bronze as a traditional sculptural material.

Morvah 1989
Bronze 22.8 x 68.5 cm
Private collection

reduction of form. A contemplative and immeasurable act, this 'crafting' of rough bronze becomes a statement of artistic integrity (a working process he employs with all materials). This has recently been a much debated issue in the interpretation of Brancusi's use of 'shine' in the 1920s.[9] However, Mitchell was also adhering to Hepworth's edict that purity of form could only be realised through an empathy with one's materials, 'by the constant exchange of touch and perception and not mechanical means'.[10]

Despite casting up to seven editions in bronze and occasionally aluminium, each work would therefore be unique. In the early 1960s Mitchell's casts were particularly unrefined, and often had to be drilled and plugged where air-holes in the sand mould had deeply pitted the cast. *Praze* had nearly one hundred holes requiring rivets before the surface was ground, filed, sanded and polished.[11] Works such as *Thrust* recast in 1992 and the recently cast *Morvah* have a much sharper, refined appearance to them as casting and finishing processes became more advanced.

In 1968 the Foreign Office commissioned Mitchell to make a new cast of *Zelah* 1961, a convoluted single form over seven feet tall to be presented to the University of the Andes in Colombia. Having joined Marjorie Parr Galleries in 1969, Mitchell could finally work on his sculpture full time. Consequently, he was able to make a trip to Bogotá two years later to teach at the university and complete a four-week lecture tour across Colombia.

At the turn of the decade, there appears a conscious absorption of historic South American references in the bronzes. Some titles such as *Solaris* (1968), *Tumarco* (1970), *Cordobda* (1971) and *Cauca* (1971), certainly suggest this.

9 *Ibid* p3

10 Barbara Hepworth article published in Penwith Society of Arts Broadsheet, *PS4* Summer 1953

11 Sand casting as opposed to the 'lost wax method' requires the original plaster form to be simple with no undercuts. It also gives a result which is roughly finished with uneven shrinkage on cooling. The process is less expensive by comparison to the lost wax method, though the latter makes for a near perfect cast.

Solaris II 1987 (second *version*) (reverse)
Bronze 45.7 x 38.1 x 12.7 cm
Family collection

Larmona 1969
Bronze 54.6 x 21.6 x 12.7 cm
Courtesy of the Stanley Picker
Private Collection

Solaris II 1987 (second *version*) (front)
Bronze 45.7 x 38.1 x 12.7 cm
Family collection

A number of works have a horizontal orientation spanning from a semi-circular space which inescapably recalls the landscape or stylised bird wings. Their motivation is likely to have been pre-Columbian jewellery; elaborate gold nose ornaments or zoomorphic 'winged' pendants made by the Yotoco or Tolima peoples who inhabited and mined the Northern Andes region in the first to seventh centuries.[12] Mitchell had in fact made jewellery alongside sculpture in the previous decade.[13]

The halo-like *Solaris* (1968) (larger second version made in 1987) typifies other works of this period, distinguished by the sculptor's exploration of patina and texture, complemented by raised sections or circular indentations of polished bronze on flattened forms. However, the earthy surface of *Probus* (1971) is animated on a larger scale by the polished edges of its angular protrusions. The shine becomes a graphic device in both of these sculptures as edge is encapsulated by dense patina, again reminiscent of the surface of slate reliefs.

12 A large collection of historic Mexican and pre-Columbian jewellery exists at the Metropolitan Museum in New York

13 Telephone conversation with Tommy Rowe 2-11-04

Opposite
Cauca 1971
Bronze 25.4 x 119.4 x 14.5 cm
Tate

Above
Probus 1971 (third cast)
Bronze 40 x 102 cm
Private collection, London

The interrelation of ideas in different media is evident from the 1960s onwards. Through its limitations, bronze gave the artist a vocabulary, which paradoxically he used again for carvings in wood and stone.[14] Thus a bronze single form *Paphos* (1974) relates to the lignum vitae wood work *Agros* of the same year and the form reoccurs again in yew wood in the 1980s. Or the graphic principles explored in slate relief are manifested in three dimensions in works such as *Skiddaw* (1974), an incised, balanced solid form made from Honister slate.

This is also a corollary of the sculptor's mode of working, surrounded in his studio by an archive of his work, natural objects and collected tools; artefacts which could lead to a progression or re-visitation of an idea. The process was no doubt aided by his move in 1967 to John Well's spacious studio at Trewarveneth School in Newlyn. With an increased schedule of shows and the demand for more space, sharing the converted school-house enabled Mitchell to undertake projects of even greater scale. Notably, this included preparing for a British Council international tour (1973-79)[15] and the fabrication

14 Tate Gallery Archive: Interview with David Lewis and Sarah Fox-Pitt 10/04/81 TAV: 249A

15 As part of its foreign policy, the British Council had set up several extensive international tours promoting British abstract artists in the post-war period. Mitchell's tour included *Gew Form* (1960), *Lamorna* (1969) and *Probus* (1971)

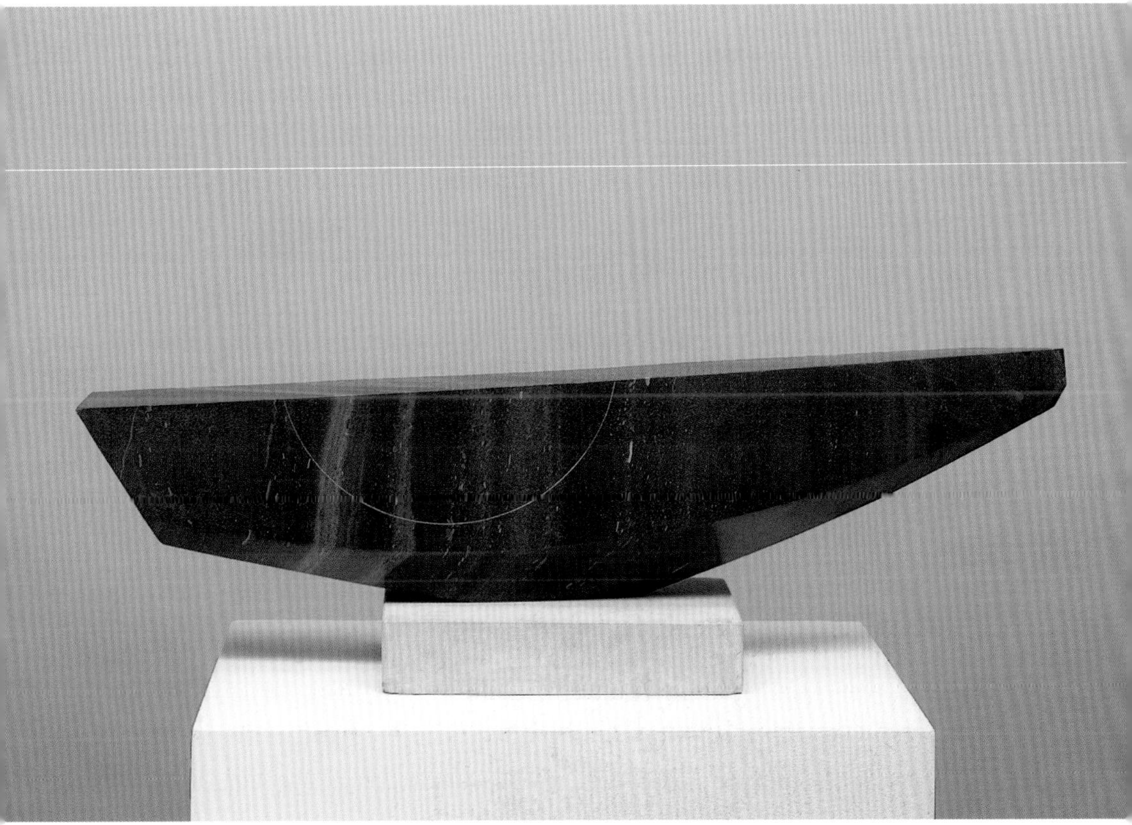

Skiddaw 1978
Honister slate 30 x 86 x 16 cm
Family collection courtesy Flowers East

of *Gemini* (1973), an exterior private commission of two eight-foot interrelated forms in Mocca Cream marble. Continuing to work in pale stone, Mitchell made a number of loosely geometric forms (of a more domestic, table-top size) the following year, including the Portland stone work *Zagcone* (1974). Like the series in Honister slate, and in addition to *Agros* made in *lignum vitae* wood at the same time, Mitchell's focus is on the formal potential of various materials, contemplating multiple possibilities within the limitations of solid form.

These explorations reflect Mitchell's reference to the classical tradition. *Zagcone* in particular, an inverted conoid, assumes an uncompromising purity. The simple balance of line and form demonstrates a satisfying 'contraposta', the subtle asymmetry prevalent throughout Mitchell's sculpture.[16] But it brings to mind Mitchell's comment on Ben Nicholson's white reliefs being 'the final statement of inspired simplicity'. Both Hepworth and Nicholson's output in the 1930s embodied this hybrid of modernist and classical ideals, which must have been recalled by the sculptor. His closer proximity to friend John Wells, who had inspired *Turning Form* in 1959 through his formally constructed compositions, may also have prompted this enquiry; the artists were to exhibit together at Plymouth City Art Gallery in 1975, although by that time Wells had essentially retired.

Mitchell's own final statements of inspired simplicity were a series of polished slate forms such as *Carnon* (1984-5). Returning in the mid 1980s to carve Delabole slate, these free-standing, flattened forms were mounted on complementary plinths of slate or stone. The works celebrate the natural beauty of the material, often maintaining a simple dialogue with geometric incisions marked by textural contrasts. Redolent of memorial stones or the

16 Giles Auty in exh. cat *A Retrospective – Sculptures 1951-90*, Gillian Jason Gallery, 1990

Agros 1974
Lignum vitae
83.8 x 21.6 x 20.3 cm
Family collection

Zagcone 1974
Portland stone
51 x 38.5 x 38.5 cm
Collection of Frank Manzi

archetypal monolith, they seem to engage with a more universal spiritual iconography popular again in post-war Britain.[17]

As opposed to the eternally dynamic nature of the bronze surface, the clean-cut slate absorbs the gaze, promoting quiet introspection. Conceivably, this denotes the sobriety of an artist working at the later stages of his career. A fact that may also explain his review and recasting of bronzes throughout the 1980s from his archive of 1960s designs.

Mitchell continued to work to his eightieth year, fabricating works with the assistance of Tommy Rowe who had latterly become 'his hands'. Since the 1960s Mitchell had worked with friends and colleagues including Breon O'Casey and William Hodge realising large commissions, tours and retrospective exhibitions in addition to finishing large castings and carvings.

It was most appropriate, that Mitchell had his last major retrospective at the Penwith Galleries, St Ives in 1992, which drew together over one hundred of his drawings, paintings and sculptures from 1932 onwards. Whilst it reaffirmed Mitchell's place in the evolution of post-war Modernism in St Ives, it celebrated his ultimate pursuit of universal forms conveying formal and philosophical enquiries in response to landscape. The combination of which may not solely be about the attainment of beauty, although his intuitive crafting of materials, above all bronze, could promote this quality. It is rather about, as Henry Moore and Bernard Leach both described, that an object should possess 'spiritual vitality', a truth that is beyond reminiscence or pure sensuality. Imbued with this sense of optimism Mitchell's significant forms are timeless in appeal but very much conduits of his time and place.

Sara Hughes is a curator at Tate St Ives

17 It brings to mind the ecclesiastic aesthetic of the new Coventry Cathedral built in the late 1960s, for example, which embodies many of its spiritual references through the medium of abstract or Modern designs by John Piper, Graham Sutherland, Jacob Epstein.

Carnon 1984
Delabole slate 59.7 x 22.8 x 20.3 cm
Family collection

Biography

1912
Born June 30th in Wealdstone, Middlesex

1913
Mother, Denis and brother Endell live with uncle in Mumbles, Swansea

1928-30
Joins The Little Theatre amateur theatre group; undertakes various odd jobs in post-war depression; attends evening classes at art school in Swansea for a couple of terms prior to moving to Cornwall.

1930
Moves to St Ives to renovate aunt's cottage in Balnoon, Halsetown with brother, Endell to set up a market garden; begins to paint more seriously

1935
Travels to Gibralter and Tangier with Endell to paint

1938
Endell takes over the Castle Inn in Fore Street and later exhibits many of the St Ives Modernist artists and it becomes a meeting place for artists

1939
Marries local girl, Jane Stevens

1940
Birth of daughter Jennifer

1942-5
Works in Geevor tin mines during the war in Home Guard with Bernard Leach and Adrian Stokes

1945
Birth of second daughter Denise

1946-8
Continues market gardening and also makes sea fishing trips; joins St Ives Society of Arts

1947
Exhibits paintings at G R Downings bookshop in Fore Street and Castle Inn

1949
Recommended by Bernard Leach becomes Barbara Hepworth's chief assistant for the following decade and she inspires his move from figurative painting to abstract sculpture; Along with other Modernists resigns from St Ives Society of Arts and becomes a founder Member of Penwith Society of Arts with Sven Berlin, John Wells, Wilhelmina Barns-Graham et al (nineteen artists in total)

1953
Funded by Ben Nicholson attends exhibition of Mexican art at Tate

1954
Birth of youngest daughter Judith

1955-7
Chairman of Penwith Society of Arts

1957-60
Makes jewellery and Porthia textile prints using designs from artists in St Ives circle to support family

1958
Completes first work in bronze

1960-7
Teaches art part-time at Penzance Grammar School and later at Redruth School of Art to support family and practice

1967
Joins Marjorie Parr Galleries and subsequently makes work full-time; shares Trewarveneth Studio in Newlyn with John Wells for the following 25 years

1968
British Foreign Office sculpture commission Zelah I, 1961 presented to University of the Andes, Bogotá, Columbia

Biography continued

1969
Acquires house in Newlyn

1970
Travels to Columbia on a lecture tour; teaches for a month at the University of the Andes in Bogotá

1973
Joins Board of Governors at Plymouth Art College

1977
Joins Board of Governors at Falmouth College of Art

1980-93
Works with assistant Tommy Rowe at Trewarveneth Studios

1993
Died 23rd March

Solo Exhibitions

1957
AIA Gallery, London

1958
Drian Gallery

1961
Waddington Galleries, London

1962
Redfern Gallery, London; Devorah Sherman Gallery, Chicago

1963
Bianchini Gallery, New York

1967
Arnolfini Gallery, Bristol; Marjorie Parr Galleries, London

1968
Richard Demarco Gallery, Edinburgh

1969
Marjorie Parr Galleries, London

1971
Marjorie Parr Galleries, London

1972
Oxford Gallery, Oxford

1973
National Museum, Malta; Compass Gallery, Glasgow

1973-9
British Council Touring exhibition: Malta, Cyprys, Greece, Yugoslavia, Malaysia, Indonesia, New Zealand and Korea

1974
City Art Gallery, Plymouth; Oxford Gallery, Oxford

1977
Alwin Gallery Grafton Street, London

1978
Festival Gallery, Bath

1979
Retrospective exhibition at Glynn Vivian Art Gallery

1987
Gillian Jason Gallery, London

1990
Gillian Jason Gallery, London

1992
Drawings Paintings and Sculpture 1932-92, Penwith Galleries, St Ives; Falmouth Art Gallery; New Ashgate Gallery Farnham

1993
Flowers East, London

1994
Memorial Exhibition Glynn Vivian Art Gallery, Swansea

1994
Kettles Yard, Cambridge; Gardener Arts Centre, University of Sussex

Group Exhibitions

1949
Penwith Society, St Ives on going

1951
Fifteen Artists and Craftsmen from St Ives Heal's Mansard Gallery and Abstract Art AIA Gallery

1958
Drian Gallery

1971-2
Selection from Arts Council Collection by Bryan Robertson, touring show

1976
Three Sculptors, Newlyn Orion Gallery

1985
St Ives 1939-64 group survey exhibition at Tate; Newlyn Art Gallery

1986
Crane Kalman Gallery with painter Patrick Hayman

1987
Looking West Newlyn Art Gallery group touring show;

1989
St Ives – Newlyn Berkeley Square Gallery with Terry Frost and Tony O'Malley;
A Century of Art in Cornwall 1889-1989, Cornwall County Council, Truro

1992
Artists from Cornwall, Royal West of England Academy, Bristol

1993
Tate St Ives inaugural show

1997
Denis Mitchell and Friends with Tony and Jane O'Malley, Connor and Nancy Fallon, and Breon O'Casey, The Bridge Gallery, Dublin

Collections

Tate, London

National Gallery of New South Wales, Sydney

The National Gallery of Wellington, New Zealand

Arts Council England

The Calouste Gulbenkian Foundation

The Walker Art Gallery Liverpool

The National Museum of Wales

Bishop Otter College, Chichester

The Cornwall Education Committee

LCC Batersea Training College

University of Manchester

Somerville College, Oxford

West Riding Education Committee

City Art Gallery, Exeter

The Royal Academy of Music, London

The Stanley Picker Trust

Camden Library Arts Dept, London

The Fitzwilliam Museum, Cambridge

Churchill College, Cambridge

The University of Leicester